YOUR KNOWLEDGE HAS VALUE

- We will publish your bachelor's and master's thesis, essays and papers

- Your own eBook and book - sold worldwide in all relevant shops

- Earn money with each sale

Upload your text at www.GRIN.com
and publish for free

Bibliographic information published by the German National Library:

The German National Library lists this publication in the National Bibliography; detailed bibliographic data are available on the Internet at http://dnb.dnb.de .

This book is copyright material and must not be copied, reproduced, transferred, distributed, leased, licensed or publicly performed or used in any way except as specifically permitted in writing by the publishers, as allowed under the terms and conditions under which it was purchased or as strictly permitted by applicable copyright law. Any unauthorized distribution or use of this text may be a direct infringement of the author s and publisher s rights and those responsible may be liable in law accordingly.

Imprint:

Copyright © 2017 GRIN Verlag
Print and binding: Books on Demand GmbH, Norderstedt Germany
ISBN: 9783668641549

This book at GRIN:

https://www.grin.com/document/413245

Susan Bailey

Terrorists within UK prison systems

A Discussion

GRIN Verlag

GRIN - Your knowledge has value

Since its foundation in 1998, GRIN has specialized in publishing academic texts by students, college teachers and other academics as e-book and printed book. The website www.grin.com is an ideal platform for presenting term papers, final papers, scientific essays, dissertations and specialist books.

Visit us on the internet:

http://www.grin.com/

http://www.facebook.com/grincom

http://www.twitter.com/grin_com

Terrorists in prison is a highly emotive topic, often filled with myths and profound political controversy, alongside tales of abuse, negligence, risk and mismanagement (Silke, 2014). Crenshaw (1992) defined the term terrorism as, a particular style of political violence, using a small number of victims to influence and scare a wider audience. As many different types of terrorist come under this umbrella, this essay will focus on one type of terrorist, the violent religious extremist group, Isis. This essay will evaluate the statement, by abolitionists, that prisons are irrational and counterproductive in relation to terrorists. This will be done by firstly evaluating critical issues around management strategies, risk assessment and the reform of imprisoned terrorists. Also, the risk of further radicalisation and de radicalisation will be explored, emphasising on the risk of keeping such prisoners. This essay will then discuss whether these strategies are successful and if not, this essay will then examine if theories of punishment can be applied to the terrorist. Her Majesty's Prison Service (HMPS) has aims that are crystallised in the HMPS statement 'Her Majesty's Prison Service serves the public by keeping in custody those committed by the courts, our duty is to look after them with humanity and help them lead law abiding and useful lives in custody after release' (Gibson, 2009). However, HMPS may be able to work towards keeping this promise in regard to other prisoners but, terrorism is different from other types of crime and many terrorists are violent extremists who cause formidable challenges (Silke, 2014). Their management can pose exceptionally difficult problems in the prison setting.

The attacks of September 11th in America were a trigger worldwide for countries to re-evaluate their counter terrorism strategies and laws, with terrorist attacks escalating across the globe from 2001-2017, claiming more than 96,000 lives (Webber,2016). The Terrorism Act 2000, was forced to be updated in 2006. Much of the counter terrorism legislation produced was aimed at Al- Qaeda, however in 2006, an equally dangerous, if not more violent group was emerging, Da'esh or ISIS. They captured territory in Iraq and Syria in 2014 and announced an establishment of Caliphate, not content with mass slaughter, rape and the enslavement of women, ISIS honed another trademark, the brutal killings of all non-believers (Webber, 2016). Governments and criminal justice systems are now faced with many new dangers and challenges posed by ISIS, such as; returning fighters from Iraq, external radicalised supporters or internal home grown radicalised supporters. As active terrorists do not seem to fear the prospect of arrest, trial or punishment, many countries have resorted to pre-emptive counter terrorism methods to protect the public such as, surveillance and pre-emptive imprisonment (Webber,2016). However, society now lives in the age of enlightenment with a stronger moral obligation to live according to humanitarian principles, some people disagree about the morality of punishment and imprisonment at all (Tunick, 1992). The public however, have a right to safety from dangerous offenders, and it should be acknowledged that prisons are unlike other communities in that they maintain a barrier to social intercourse with the world outside for the public's safety (Staniforth et al., 2013). In the beginning of the 1990's there were many radical thoughts and suggestions that prisons ought to be abolished, a government white paper was published in 1990 that stated that prisons were little more than costly universities (Othmani and Bessi, 2008). It was claimed by abolitionists that prison was not a positive solution and only contributed to the criminalisation of society. Encouraging those who were already rotten to become worse, however this statement has not considered the impact on public safety, which has become an issue of high priority with regards to the increasing number of violent religious extremists within the UK (Othmani and Bessi, 2008). The central theme of general abolitionism is that punishment is never justified and argues that the whole criminal justice system is a social problem that needs to be dismantled and replaced with a new system, however, abolitionists have not stated what this new system will consist of (Lilly et al., 2015). Therefore, prisons are now adapting and modernising to meet the demands of the added pressure they find themselves under.

The UK penal system has found itself under increasing pressure to try and develop strategies, policies and interventions to accommodate the growing number of extremist prisoners within its walls (Silke, 2014). Between September 2001 and March 2016, there were 1,150 prisoners charged with terrorist related offences (Grimwood, 2016). The counter Terrorism and Security Act (2015) stated that all public-sector organisations are subject to a duty to prevent people from being drawn to terrorism, however, in 2016 over 1000 prisoners displayed behaviours that raised concerns (Grimwood, 2016). A government report published in October 2015 contained comments made by David Cameron, who described the fight against extremism as one of the greatest struggles of our generation and suggested that prisons must now wake up and accept responsibility for previous years and poor choices (Grimwood, 2016). This responsibility has mainly fallen on the National Offender Management strategy (NOMS), who have developed a series of strategies that can be used regarding these prisoners. The prison service extremist unit has also become a part of NOMS, established in 2007 with the responsibility of developing strategies, policies and procedures appropriate to the risks presented by terrorists (Walker and Lennon, 2015). The first specialist branch to deal with counter terrorism in the mid 60's only consisted of around 300 officers in the UK, by 1978, the force was 1,638 strong and in 2003, it consisted of 4,247 officers, the number of specialist officers in counter terrorism, by demand is a growing number (Wilkinson, 2007). New risk assessment measures have also been created, such as the violent extremist risk assessment (VERA), which is specifically used for ideologically motivated offenders (Silke, 2014). The most dominant response to the imprisonment of violent extremists is focussed on intelligence gathering, risk assessment and risk management (Walker and Lennon, 2015). Amongst the range of new programmes aimed specifically at violent extremists is a form of cognitive behavioural therapy (CBT), which is based on the principle of exposing extremists to mainstream Islam (Veldhuis, 2009). This exposure is facilitated through meeting experienced and respected Islamic scholars, paying attention to the radical extremist's version and interpretation (Silke, 2014). A study conducted in America by the United States Senate revealed that on average over 80% of prisoners will turn to Islam when converting to a faith whilst in prison (Mulcahy et al., 2013). Therefore, religious counselling is now recognised as a powerful instrument for offender reform, it can encourage the offender to adhere to a more peaceful, moderate religious interpretation, that does not legitimize terrorist activities (Veldhuis, 2009). CBT aims to focus on the understanding and changing of cognitive processes to try and improve abstract thinking, critical reasoning and to encourage goal setting (Veldhuis, 2009). Group discussions, on the job training, parole and probation, individual classifications and needs assessments, social and recreational activities and financial aftercare are several other components of rehabilitation programmes offered by the prison service (Gunaratna and Bin Ali, 2015). Prison rehabilitation is a complex issue, one that will ideally consist of a number of experts working together, such as, psychologists, social workers, religious experts and prison officers in order to achieve a successful rehabilitation or reform (Gunaratna and Bin Ali, 2015). Claims of success have varied, and so far, there are only recordings of successful rehabilitation through intervention programmes that have been used on 'soft- core' extremists (Silke, 2011).

However, the workings and success of these rehabilitation programmes are heavily affected by the individual involved, some of the most committed extremists referred to as 'irreconcilables' are not receptacle to reform at all (Veldhuis, 2009). In these cases, risk is considered more important, with little attention to the role of rehabilitation (Walker and Lennon, 2015). Prison officials will want to deter, disrupt and detect all communications that would benefit a terrorist's objective (Gunaratna and Bin Ali, 2015). The UK prison system has a unique way of managing terrorists that differs from The Netherlands, USA and Australia, in UK prisons terrorists are not held separately and are dispersed into the prison population (Jones, 2014). Learning from past experiences with IRA prisoners the UK government are reluctant to categorise and separate terrorists as they found that the segregation promoted solidarity and unity within the extremist group, it made them stronger (Jones, 2014). Terrorists are held in category A prisons, where they are subject to extra supervision, restricted movements and socialising with others, extra searches, and regular cell changes (Jones, 2014).

Although this may seem inhumane towards the prisoner it is good recognition from the prison service that standard risk assessment will not be sufficient to protect the public (Silke, 2014). Alongside the prisons duty to protect the public from violent extremists it is also important that all restrictions placed by prison officials will be applicable to domestic and international law, including the international covenant of civil and political rights (ICCPR) (Gunaratna and Bin Ali, 2015). One of the stated aims of the HMPS is to protect the public and most violent religious extremists pose an immediate danger to the public (Staniforth et al., 2013). This is because of many factors, such as, the global reach of extremists, the immediacy of danger from self-starting groups or lone actors and their total disregard for fundamental human rights. Prison has been, quite often, the very context in which violent action is pondered, produced and planned (Wieviorka, 2004). This assumption is based on a few high-profile cases such as, Kevin James, Levar Washington and Richard Reid, the infamous shoe bomber who converted to Islam and planned a terrorist attack from inside the prison walls (Wilkinson, 2007). Reid attempted to detonate a bomb on board a passenger plane, claiming that he had become radicalised whilst in prison. These prisoners gave justification for the Government to label all terrorists as high-risk offenders, which led to the public viewing prisons as schools of crime for terrorists, resulting in costly rehabilitation programmes and interventions (Jones, 2014).

These types of 'high risk 'prisoners can cause serious implications within a prison setting, such as the evidence of various terrorist factions sharing information, training and intelligence whilst imprisoned. Peer to peer radicalisation has been identified as a contributing factor fuelling extremism, the prisons aims to combat extremism is just one strand of the Governments counter extremist strategy (Grimwood, 2016). The UK prison system can be used as a source of recruitment, with a growing prison population, it can create an environment characterised by individuals who resent the British authorities and the system, therefore, creating conditions conductive to recruitment (Wilkinson, 2007). When an individual is imprisoned it is common for the individual to experience both physical and emotional trauma, making them much more vulnerable and impressionable (Mulcahy et al., 2013). At the beginning of their imprisonment acute and chronic stress related factors such as sleep loss, loss of appetite and the magnification of the pains of imprisonment that Sykes (1958) identified, can give recruiters a perfect opportunity to assess the prisoner's vulnerability and the likeliness of them conforming to their extremist groups (Mulcahy et al., 2013).

The prison service must be concerned about radicalisation of other prisoners, which can result in an 'ordinary' prisoner becoming much more dangerous upon release (Silke, 2014). A report by the International Centre for the Study of Radicalisation and Political Violence at Kings College, London, revealed harrowing results, suggesting that prisons were breeding grounds for radicalisation, and that overcrowding and under staffing were to blame (Grimwood, 2016). The report went on to further suggest that prisons were emphasising on security first and were missing opportunities to reform. However, if the terrorist population consists mainly of 'irreconcilables' then security must become the prisons priority to uphold the original promise of public protection. The process of radicalisation is poorly understood due to the limited amount of information researchers can obtain, it is a very secret organisation with cleverly organised methods of recruitment, however, this lack of knowledge can obstruct new developments in attempting to solve, manage and reduce this issue (Mulcahy et al., 2013).

Other findings and studies of UK prisons contradict the 'school of crime and recruitment theory', as UK prisons all have their own individual culture, religious and political characteristics (Jones, 2014). It has been found in prisons where Muslim population is low the recruitment and radicalisation process may be inhibited and can provide temporary disengagement of terrorist offenders, therefore making the prison experience productive. Further to this, the UK prison system has seen a separation of Muslim prisoners from Non-Muslim offenders, partly due to the westernised perception that Islam is dangerous, backwards and 'other' (Jones, 2014). There is evidence that hostility is growing within prisons, with Islamophobia raising tensions to the level where terrorist prisoners are vulnerable and are experiencing violence and exclusion from the prison population (Liebling et al., 2011). The media perception of Islam and ongoing occurrences involving terrorist attacks directed at western interests have resulted in a rise of retaliatory action inside prisons, making the desire to join extremist's groups unpopular (Liebling et al., 2011). Therefore, it is highly unlikely that an ordinary prisoner will become radicalised within a western prison, significantly reducing the level of threat from the imprisoned terrorist and significantly improving public safety whilst they are imprisoned.

There are many theories that can be applied to why punishment is necessary or justified, with many people who do not agree with punishment at all. Theories such as deterrence theory or incapacitation theory can provide some explanation as to why prison is necessary, however, it is difficult to apply these to prisoners such as 'irreconcilables'. General deterrence is used to set an example to others who may be considering committing the same crime, relying on the basis that an offender's punishment should be sufficient to prevent future instances of the offence (Darley et al., 2002). However, this theory is based on the presumption that the offender is a rational actor, it has been proven that in the case of the violent extremist, they do not hold rational beliefs and are subject to ideologies (Ankersen, 2008). The violent religious extremist is a complex phenomenon and is little understood, it is also unclear as to how to neutralize the number of recruits who follow them or how to stop them attacking the pubic (Ankerson, 2008). However, attacks still must be stopped to protect public safety, therefore, the removal of a convicted offender from the community, through imprisonment, using incapacitation is recommended (Zimring and Hawkins, 1997). Violent actors who have the intention and the capacity to cause harm or death must be detained, however, using incapacitation is to predict future behaviour, which is not always considered morally correct (Bjorgo, 2013). Upon measuring the success of incapacitation, it is quite simple, Bentham (1811), stated that, for a body to act, it must be there, however, the cost of keeping a prisoner indefinitely is too much for the prison system to realistically manage. There is also the exception to the theory, Richard Reid, who planned an attack whilst inside prison and the further thought that incapacitation may reinforce anger and hostility, therefore not reducing the threat in the long term (Bjorgo, 2013).

The relationship between imprisonment and crime levels is a complex topic, with a high level of reoffending in the UK. To keep prisoners indefinitely costs around £45,000 per year, per prisoner and with no guarantee of reduced recidivism rates, holding prisoners for longer is becoming an economic burden (Easton and Piper, 2016). Extensive research has suggested that the reduction in crime through imprisonment is very small, around 5%, this is understood to be because punishment is only one factor linked to criminality (Easton and Piper, 2016). Therefore, applying theories of punishment such as deterrence and incapacitation to the violent extremist may not be productive, with high levels of critique around rational choice and economic implications for each theory. However, although the need to continually reassess the counter terrorism policies, theories and strategies is present, the pre-emptive and incapacitated imprisonment of terrorists remains an important counter terrorism tool. There are crucial differences between terrorism crimes and domestic crimes, domestic crimes are usually committed for personal gain whereas terrorist crimes are to target the state, or directly agents of the state (Salinas de fras, 2014). Terrorist crimes have the intention of committing indiscriminate attacks on the general public with murderous intent, and whilst terrorists may commit vehicle theft or identity theft in order to aid their terrorist plot, the overarching objectives, and resultant impact, are fundamentally different (Salinas de fras, 2014). The primary reason that imprisonment, using pre-emptive strategic methods, carried out by the prison staff is important, is because it can prevent terrorists from inflicting a scale of public harm that far outweighs the level of public harm a domestic criminal is prepared to inflict (Salinas de fras, 2014). The abolition of prisons has been heavily criticized for being to 'impractical' and a danger to the public for being imprecise, with no clear plan of action other than close the prisons (Lilly et al., 2015). Abolitionists lack a well-grounded theory and are often described as 'vision without strategy', therefore emphasising that prison is required for the violent religious extremist as the prison system has a vision and a strategy in place.

Whilst prison is thought to encourage radicalisation amongst ordinary prisoners, studies by Leibling (2011) have demonstrated that in a western prison, they rarely have that effect. The terrorist is now becoming subjected to fear, exclusion and isolation from other inmates, due to the clever strategies developed by the prison system. Prisons have modernised and adapted and introduced new training for staff and have introduced new policies and reform techniques to manage these difficult prisoners, therefore making the imprisonment of terrorists a safer option for wider society. Specialised forces are growing and have more than doubled in numbers to meet the needs to ensure public safety. Prison does reduce the terrorism threat in the short term, the system simply cannot wait whilst bombs are exploding in public places, causing fear, moral panic, general anxiety and death (Bjorgo, 2013). Prison is also necessary to halt the terrorism threat in the here and now, regardless of there not being a clear solution as to what works, or the threat of prison being a school of crime (Bjorgo, 2013). The harm these offenders cause within the prison walls is significantly less than if they were in the community. Despite some theorists accusing prisons of being counterproductive and irrelevant, they are overlooking the fact that, they do separate dangerous offenders from the wider society and the main point is that terrorist violence is a different, more dangerous form of crime, and it should be treated as such (Bjorgo, 2013). Whilst applying the full repertoire of crime prevention mechanisms, strategies and measures, prisons are now vital to reduce the immediate threat in order to protect public safety. One of the prisons deliberate purposes is to separate inmates on behalf of the wider society. The question must be asked, what the implications for public safety are, if it did not. The abolition of prison has not been researched critically enough and there are no other practical plans for how to manage dangerous offenders without the prison system. Therefore, to ensure the public's safety from these violent religious extremists intent on causing mass destruction and death, it is imperative that they remain in prison until rehabilitated, even if rehabilitation is not always guaranteed, it will reduce the amount of death and destruction they will cause if they had the freedom to do so.

Alex Conte. (2010). *Human Rights in the Prevention and Punishment of Terrorism*. [Place of publication not identified]: Springer-Verlag Berlin Heidelberg.

Ankersen, C. (2008). *Understanding global terror*. Cambridge [u.a.]: Polity Press.

Bjørgo, T. (2013). *Strategies for preventing terrorism*. Basingstoke [u.a.]: Palgrave.

Bjørgo, T. (2007). *Root causes of terrorism*. Enskede: TPB.

Darley, J., Carlsmith, K. and Robinson, P. (2000). Incapacitation and just deserts as motives for punishment. *Law and Human Behavior*, 24(6), pp.659-683.

Easton, S. and Piper, C. (2016). *Sentencing and punishment*. Oxford: Oxford University Press.

Gibson, B. (2009). *The pocket A-Z of criminal justice*. Hampshire, UK: Waterside Press.

Gibson, B., Cavadino, P. and Faulkner, D. (2008). *The criminal justice system*. Winchester: Waterside Press.

Gunaratna, R. and Bin Ali, M. (2015). *Terrorist rehabilitation*. London: Imperial College Press.

House of commons library (2016). *Radicalisation in prisons in England and Wales*.

Jones, C. (2014). Are prisons really schools for terrorism? Challenging the rhetoric on prison radicalization. *Punishment & Society*, 16(1), pp.74-103.

Mulcahy, E., Merrington, S. and Bell, P. (2013). The Radicalisation of Prison Inmates: A Review of the Literature on Recruitment, Religion and Prisoner Vulnerability. *Journal of Human Security*, 9(1).

Othmani, A. and Bessis, S. (2008). *Beyond prison*. New York: Berghahn Books.

Salinas De Fras, A., Salinas de Frías, A., Samuel, K. and White, N. (2014). *Counter-Terrorism*. Oxford: OUP Oxford.

Lilly, J., Ball, R. and Cullen, F. (2015). *Criminology theory*. Thousand Oaks, Calif.: SAGE.

Silke, A. (2011). *The Psychology of Counter-Terrorism*. London: Routledge.

Silke, A. (2009). *Terrorists, victims and society*. Chichester: Wiley.

Silke, A. (2014). *Prison, Terrorism and Extremism*. Hoboken: Taylor and Francis.

Staniforth, A., Ratcliffe, M., Rabenstein, C., Walker, C. and Osborne, S. (2013). *Blackstone's counter-terrorism handbook.* Oxford: Oxford University Press.

Tunick, M. (1992). *Punishment.* Berkeley: University of California Press.

Veldhuis, T. and Staun, J. (2009). *Islamist radicalisation.* The Hague: Netherlands Institute of International Relations Clingendael.

Walker, C. and Lennon, G. (2015). *Routledge handbook of law and terrorism.* Abingdon, Oxon UK: Routledge.

Webber, D. (2016). *Preventive detention of terror suspects.* London: Routledge, Taylor & Francis Group.

Wieviorka, M. (2004). *The making of terrorism.* Chicago, Ill.: University of Chicago Press.

Wilkinson, P. (2007). *Homeland security in the UK.* London: Routledge.

Zimring, F. and Hawkins, G. (1997). *Incapacitation.* New York: Oxford University Press.

YOUR KNOWLEDGE HAS VALUE

- We will publish your bachelor's and master's thesis, essays and papers

- Your own eBook and book - sold worldwide in all relevant shops

- Earn money with each sale

Upload your text at www.GRIN.com
and publish for free